Samuel Swaim Stewart

The Minstrel Banjoist

Samuel Swaim Stewart

The Minstrel Banjoist

ISBN/EAN: 9783744646888

Printed in Europe, USA, Canada, Australia, Japan

Cover: Foto ©Andreas Hilbeck / pixelio.de

More available books at **www.hansebooks.com**

THE

MINSTREL BANJOIST.

By S. S. STEWART.

Price 50 Cents.

Published by S. S. STEWART,
BANJO MANUFACTURER AND MUSIC PUBLISHER,
No. 429 N. EIGHTH STREET, Philadelphia, Pa.
COPYRIGHT, 1881, by S. S. STEWART.

. J. M. ARMSTRONG & CO., MUSIC TYPOGRAPHERS. PHILADELPHIA.

THE MINSTREL BANJOIST.

CONTAINING

THE RUDIMENTS OF MUSIC

AND

A COURSE OF INSTRUCTION FOR THE BANJO:

TOGETHER WITH

A Choice Collection

OF

➤✶ JIGS, REELS, SCHOTTISCHES, ETC.✶◄

BY

S. S. STEWART

Author of "THE YOUNG BANJOIST,"
" LESSONS AND STUDIES FOR THE BANJO,"
"THE ARTISTIC BANJOIST," "THE BANJO PLAYER'S HAND-BOOK," ETC.

Published by S. S. STEWART,

BANJO MANUFACTURER AND MUSIC PUBLISHER,

No. 429 N. Eighth Street, Philadelphia, Pa.

CONTENTS

Entered according to Act of Congress, in the year 1881, by

S. S. STEWART,

in the Office of the Librarian of Congress, at Washington, D.C.

J. M. ARMSTRONG & CO., MUSIC TYPOGRAPHERS, PHILADELPHIA.

2

MINSTREL BANJOIST.

———⟨⟩———

. INTRODUCTORY REMARKS.

A great many who take up the Banjo, do so with the idea of "having some fun with it." This· little book has been issued for such, and for those who desire to learn the Banjo for the Minstrel stage. .

Those who desire to master the higher departments of the art of Banjo playing should have such books as "The Artistic Banjoist," "The Young Banjoist," "The Banjo-player's Hand-book and Complete Instructor," "The Banjoist's Own Collection of Choice Music," and other works, together with the various lessons and studies published by the author. Therefore those who take up this work expecting to find therein the same high class of music contained in some of the author's former works may be disappointed; but the reader should recollect that all tastes are to be suited, and what pleases one may not please another. We firmly believe, however, that no person interested in our only American instrument, the Banjo, will purchase this work and feel that he has not the worth of his money.

ORGANIZING A MINSTREL TROUPE.

In organizing a minstrel company the first thing to do is to select a person who is competent to act as manager. If you attempt to start without a head to the concern, the chances are that the organization will never amount to any thing. Another suitable person should be chosen as stage manager, and another to act as treasurer. The costumes necessary may mostly be made by any ordinary tailor or seamstress. The wigs may be had of theatrical wig makers in New York, Philadelphia, Boston, or any of our large cities, and cost from one dollar upwards. For the "Comic Banjoist" a close crop silk plush wig is the best. A very large pair of shoes are also considered necessary, and these are made by theatrical boot and shoe makers, or may be made by almost any ordinary shoemaker. They should be constructed as light as possible, great weight being a decided objection. A very large pair of prison-made shoes come in handy to wear in comic negro acts, etc. These may be bought for about two dollars.

HOW TO PREPARE BURNT CORK.

Cut a quantity of champagne corks into thin shavings and satruate them with alcohol. Place them in a pan and set fire to them : they will burn into fine powder.

HOW TO "BLACK UP."

Applying cork to the face and hands is called "blacking up." First, moisten the hands with water; then take a small quantity of the powdered cork, and after rubbing well with the hands, apply to the face and neck. The eyes should be kept closed whilst applying the cork, and care should be taken that no streaks or bare places are left upon the face or neck. Finally, remove the cork from the palms of the hands with a-piece of damp paper or rag.

HOW TO REMOVE THE CORK, OR "WASH UP."

Use common washing soap, and make a heavy lather on hands (or sponge, which is generally used); after rubbing thoroughly, wash off with clean water.

"BANJO STORIES."

The minstrel banjoist generally before beginning his comic songs will introduce a " few remarks," or tell a short story in order to put his audience in a pleasant humor. Some "Banjo Soloists" are better at talking than at playing, and tire out their hearers with long and often tedious or somewhat stale "gags." The banjoist of the present day should endeavor, as much as possible, to rely upon his playing or singing, and not too much upon his "gift of gab." As a specimen of "Banjo remarks" the following, written by Mr. Harry P. Wayne, is given :—

(Enter Jake, laughing, with Banjo on shoulder.)

Spoken—Yes, I'm here. Who said I wasn't here? I just got back. Yes, I just got back. I say I just got back,—got back,—yes, got back from Leadville. Talk about towns! If that ain't the greatest town in this world! Yes, sir. I went there about three months ago. I didn't go alone. Oh, no! I had three chums,—a shoemaker and two tailors. Well, when we got out there we were going through Yunk Yunk Street, and some kid—yes, a kid,—some kid—you know a kid—why, some kid,—a kid he comes up and he says to the shoemaker, he says "Gummey, you're too fresh. I've got a good notion to pin your ears back and swallow you whole without ever"——. He never finished his unmitigated remarks. The shoemaker hit him : he dropped,—yes, he dropped, dropped down a precipice about three good feet high. Well, you may know how far he dropped. When they went to look for him they found a yaller button, belonging to his pants about one mile on this side of China. The shoemaker he was arrested, and the liar which he got to offend him made a very disgusting speech. He said it was a shame to hang that man. "Why!" he says "that man's a shoemaker,—the only one we have here,. What would we do without him?" The judge says. "That settles it: the prisoner is, discharged." So they hung one of the tailors. I'm going to sing you a little song written out there by General Grant the day after George Francis Train married Doctor Mary Walker.·

[*Plays interlude.*]

HOLDING THE BANJO

The rim should rest on the centre of the right thigh. The handle or neck should rest between the thumb and finger. The right hand is supported by the forearm resting over the top of the rim; whilst the small or little finger rests on the head to support the hand.

THE BANJO STRINGS NAMED.

The first or thinnest gut string is B; the second is G sharp; the third is E; the fourth, or silver, is A; and the fifth, or short thumb string, is E.

STRINGING THE BANJO.

For the first, or B, use a thin string that is manufactured expressly for that purpose: the same string is also used for the fifth. For the second, use a light Violin E. For the third, use a heavy Violin E, or light A. The Bass, or silver string, should be one that is wound on fine silk expressly for the Banjo.

THE RUDIMENTS OF MUSIC.

The staff or stave consists of five parallel lines and four spaces, upon which musical characters, called notes, are written :—

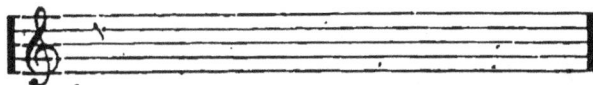

A sign, thus, 𝄞 indicates the G or Treble Clef in which Banjo Music is always written. There are two clefs in common use, the Treble clef and Bass clef. Banjo, Violin, Guitar and Flute music is always written in the Treble clef; also the right-hand parts of Piano and Organ music.
Musical notes are named after the first seven letters of the alphabet :—A, B, C, D, E, F, G.

The names of the notes on the lines are as follow :—

The names of the notes between the lines or in the spaces are as follow :—

It will be seen that the notes in the spaces spell the word F A C E, which renders them easy to remember.
When the notes extend beyond the limits of the staff, additional lines are employed called *ledger lines.*

SCALE WITH LEDGER LINES.

ON TUNING THE BANJO.

Begin with the fourth or silver string, which tune to A, or near it. (A below the staff, on piano, organ or violin.) Then stop the 4th string at the 7th fret, and tune the 3d, or thickest gut string, in unison. Then stop the 3d string at 4th fret, and tune the 2d string in unison. Then stop the 2d string at 3d fret, and tune the 1st string in unison. Then stop the 1st string at 5th fret, and tune the short 5th string in unison. After sufficient practice the ear becomes accustomed to the sounds, and it is then an easy matter to tune by ear without stopping the strings.

FRETTING THE BANJO.

All beginners on the Banjo require one that has frets. Some prefer raised frets, so that by stopping the string between the frets the string is brought down on the frets. But more proficient performers generally prefer smooth or level frets, which are used as guides. The interval of sound from the open string to the first fret and from one fret to the next one, etc., is one semitone, or half a tone. Thus, beginning with the lowest note on the Banjo, which is A, the fourth string open, the same string stopped at the second fret makes B, as the first would make A sharp or B flat, etc.

PICKING AND STRIKING THE BANJO.

There are two styles of playing the Banjo :—the first, or picking, style being the most used. Rest the little finger on the head near the bridge, pick the third, fourth and fifth strings with the thumb; pick the second string with the first finger, and the first string with second finger. After sufficient practice the pupil should learn to use three fingers by picking the third string with first finger, second string with second finger, and first string with third finger. This facilitates execution. The striking style is now mostly used for military marches, etc., and is readily mastered after the pupil has made himself familiar with the picking style.

4

THE NATURAL KEY OF THE BANJO.

By the Natural key we mean the key in which it is easiest to play. A major is considered the Natural key of the Banjo, as C major is the Natural key of the Piano.

MAJOR AND MINOR KEYS.

There are twenty-four different keys: twelve major, and twelve minor. Each major key has its relative minor key beginning a third below.

SHARPS, FLATS AND NATURALS.

A sharp, thus ♯, raises the note before which it is placed a half tone. A flat, thus ♭, lowers the note a half tone. A natural, thus ♮, cancels a flat or sharp by restoring the note to its original pitch. A double sharp, thus 𝄪 or ×, raises a note two half tones, or one full tone. A double flat lowers a note in the same manner.

THE BANJO IN TUNE.

When the banjo is in tune the open strings make the following notes :—

The 4th string. 3d string. 2d string. 1st string. 5th string.

A Banjo may, however, be tuned to a higher pitch, as is necessary for a short neck banjo; but in any case the notes are always read as though tuned as above.

TIME.

Without a knowledge of time it is impossible to perform correctly. The time or movement of any piece of music is always expressed by figures at the beginning of the piece. A piece is said to be in common or ₄ time when each bar or measure contains the value of a whole note or its equivalent in rests.

COMMON, OR ₄ TIME. Four counts in each measure.

A dot placed after a note increases its length one half. Thus in the first measure of above exercise the quarter note is dotted, and thereby increased in length to three eighths. In the last measure, as the notes only fill out ¾ of the time, a quarter rest is introduced to complete the measure.

THE TRIPLET.

A figure 3 over or under any three notes, indicates that they are to be played in the time of two notes of the same kind.

Played in the following time :—

THE VALUE OR DURATION OF NOTES.

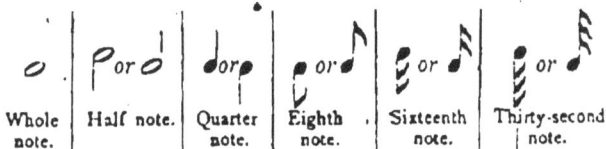

| Whole note. | Half note. | Quarter note. | Eighth note. | Sixteenth note. | Thirty-second note. |

RESTS,

Whole rest. Half rest. Quarter rest. Eighth rest. Sixteenth rest. Thirty-second rest.

TWO-FOUR TIME. Two counts in each measure.

THREE-FOUR TIME. Three counts in each measure.

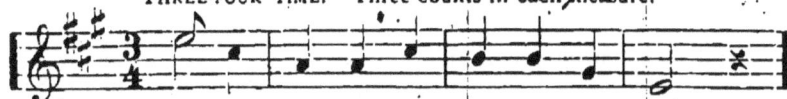

SIX-EIGHT TIME. Compound Common Time.

MUSICAL TERMS.

FINE means *the end.* D. C. stands for Da Capo, and signifies that you are to go back to beginning of the piece and play to the word *fine.* The following sign ⌒ is sometimes used in place of the word *fine.* When this is placed over a double bar, thus it denotes the end of the piece. *f* stands for FORTE, and means *loud* or *strong.* *ff* for FORTISSIMO, meaning *very loud.* *p* for PIANO, *soft.* *pp* for PIANISSIMO, *very soft.* DOLCE, *sweet.* Bls, *twice.* *fz* or ➤, means to strike suddenly and diminish rapidly. When this sign ⌒ is placed over or under a note it indicates that the time of the note is to be prolonged to suit the taste of the performer.

GRACE NOTES OR ORNAMENTS.

When small notes, as per following example, are introduced into a piece, they are put there for the purpose of embellishment, and are not counted in the time, but generally borrow their time from the following note :—

· EXAMPLE.

THE NATURAL KEY OF THE BANJO.

A MAJOR WITH THREE SHARPS.

The short 5th string makes the note E, same as on first string 5th fret. When the 5th string is to be used the note is generally designated by a double stem, thus:

Practice the foregoing scale until you can read all the notes off at sight. O stands for open string and F stands for fret. Begin with 4th string open, then 2d fret, then 4th fret, and so on. Use the second finger for second fret, then slide the same finger to fourth fret, and use the little finger for fifth fret. Always use first finger for first fret.

THE SCALE OF F SHARP MINOR, RELATIVE TO A MAJOR.

SCALE OF E MAJOR, WITH FOUR SHARPS.

SCALE OF C SHARP MINOR, RELATIVE TO B MAJOR.

ASCENDING:

C♯ D♯ E F♯ G♯ A♯ B♯ C♯

4 f.   6 f.   o   2 f.   o   2 f.   1 f.   2 f.

DESCENDING.

C♯ B A G♯ F♯ E D♯ C♯

2 f.   o   1 f.   o   2 f.   o   6 f.   4 f.

SCALE OF D MAJOR, WITH TWO SHARPS.

D E F♯ G A B C♯ D

5 f.   o   2 f.   3 f.   1 f.   o   2 f.   3 f.

SCALE OF B MINOR, RELATIVE TO D MAJOR.

ASCENDING.

2 f.   4 f.   5 f.   o   2 f.   o   2 f.   o

DESCENDING.

COMMON CHORDS OF A MAJOR.

USED FOR ACCOMPANIMENTS.

RELATIVE MINOR.

CHORDS IN E MAJOR.

RELATIVE MINOR.

CHORDS IN D MAJOR.

RELATIVE MINOR.

"THE BARRE," OR "BAR" CHORDS.

To make a barre, place the first finger of left hand firmly across the four strings and leave the other fingers free to stop the other notes.—The measure marked 5th pos. Barre, is made as follows. Place first finger across four strings at 5th fret, which makes D and A on 4th and 3d strings; then place 3d finger on 2d string at 6th fret, which makes D; then place 4th finger on 1st string at 7th fret, making F♯.

EASY JIG.

THE SNAP.

When two or more notes are united with a curved line, thus, ⌒ it generally indicates that the first note is picked as usual, and the following note is snapped off with the finger of the left hand, which is used to stop the foregoing note. The snap is used to facilitate rapid execution.

15

CHORDS IN THE "POSITIONS."

When the hand is next to the nut, or so that the first finger will fall upon the first fret, it is called "first position." The position that a chord may be in is determined by the fret which the first finger falls upon.

The figures attached to the notes indicate the fingers of the left hand, which should be used to make the notes.

A complete knowledge of the fingerboard may be obtained from "THE BANJOIST'S ASSISTANT; OR, NOTE-READING MADE EASY,"—a large chart by S. S. Stewart: price, twenty-five cents.

SCALE OF C MAJOR, WITHOUT SIGNATURE.

CHORDS IN C MAJOR.

SCALE OF A MINOR, RELATIVE TO C MAJOR.

ASCENDING.

A   B   C   D   E   F♯   G♯   A

o   2d f.   3d f.   5th f.   o   2d f.   o   1st f.

DESCENDING.

1st f.   3d f.   1st f   o   5th f.   3d f.   2d f.   o

CHORDS IN A MINOR.

17

ROARING JELLY JIG.

IRISH JIG.

THE EARLY BIRD SCHOTTISCHE.

TRIPLET CLOG SCHOTTISCHE.

B. B. B.

ANGELICA POLKA.

G. E. MACK.

DE CHARLESTON GALS.

OLD JOE'S LAMENT.—BANJO SONG.

1 { Old Joe stood at the gar - den gate :
{ You kill my dog I'll kill your cat :

2 { Old Joe he gave me some slack :
{ Den dat ole Joe he went right home :

3 { Den Old Joe went right up to bed,
{ When he snored de chil - dren run,

He couldn't get in cause he
Now mind, ole man, what
I took a stick and
With a brok-en back and a
He hauled de clothes up o-
Dey thought for sure de

OLD JOE'S LAMENT. Concluded.

came too late :·
you am at.
broke his back.
crooked Shin bone.
ver his head.
divil had cum.

REFRAIN.

Old Joe! Old Joe! Old Joe kick-ing up be-

DAKOTA JIG.

Tune Bass to B 5 f.

ED. H. HULSE.

WALK AROUND.

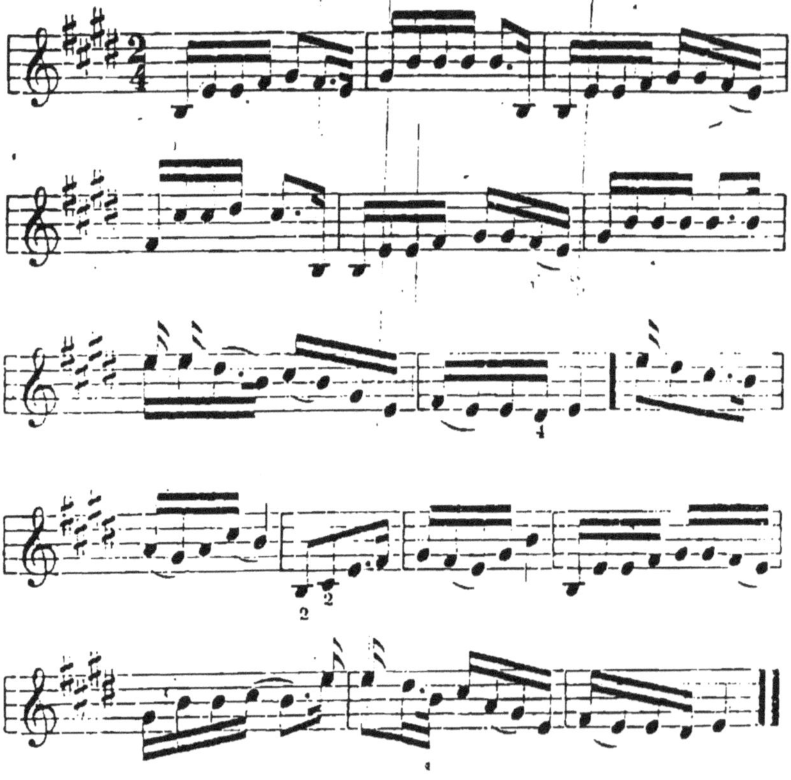

STOP JIG.

A MINOR.

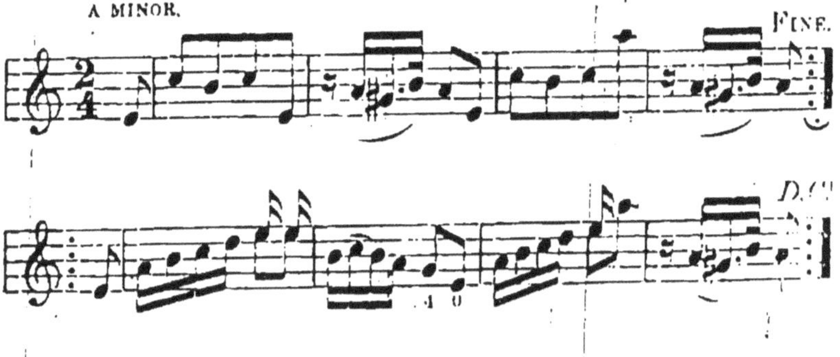

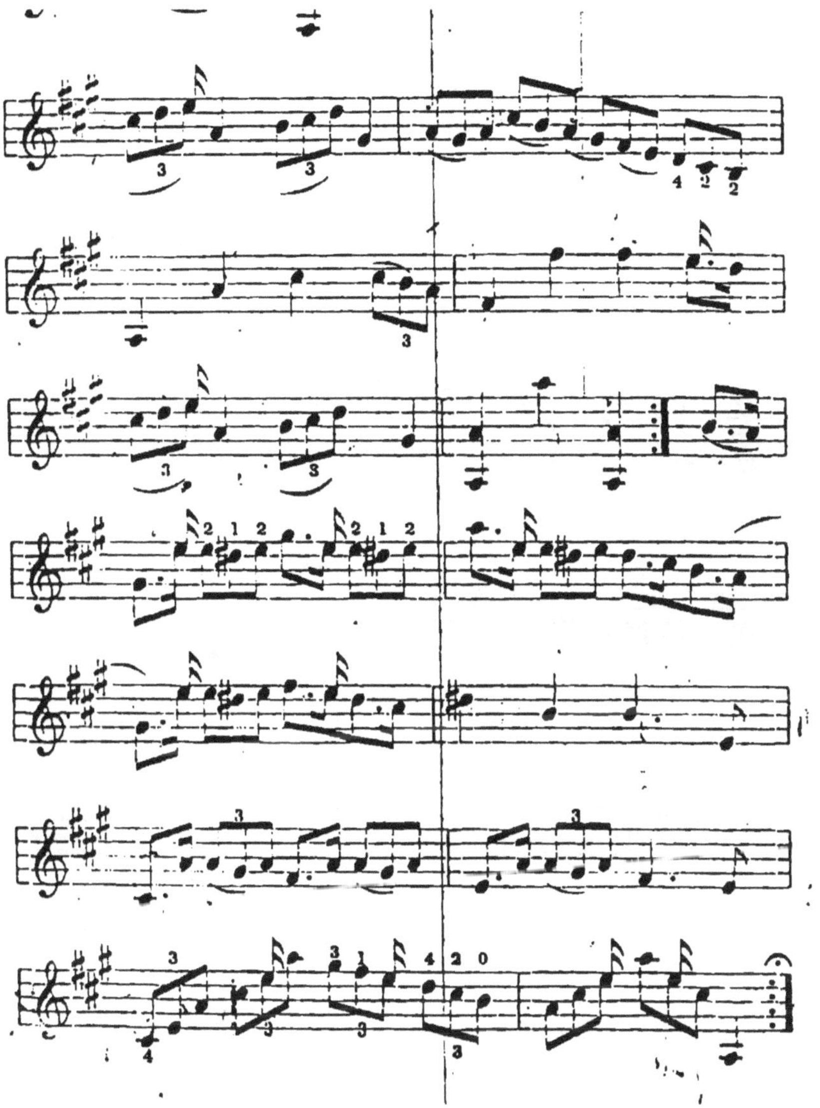

ROSEBUD REEL.

C MAJOR.

No. 1.   **QUADRILLE SET.**

Arranged by A. BAUR.

No. 2.

FINE.

D.C.

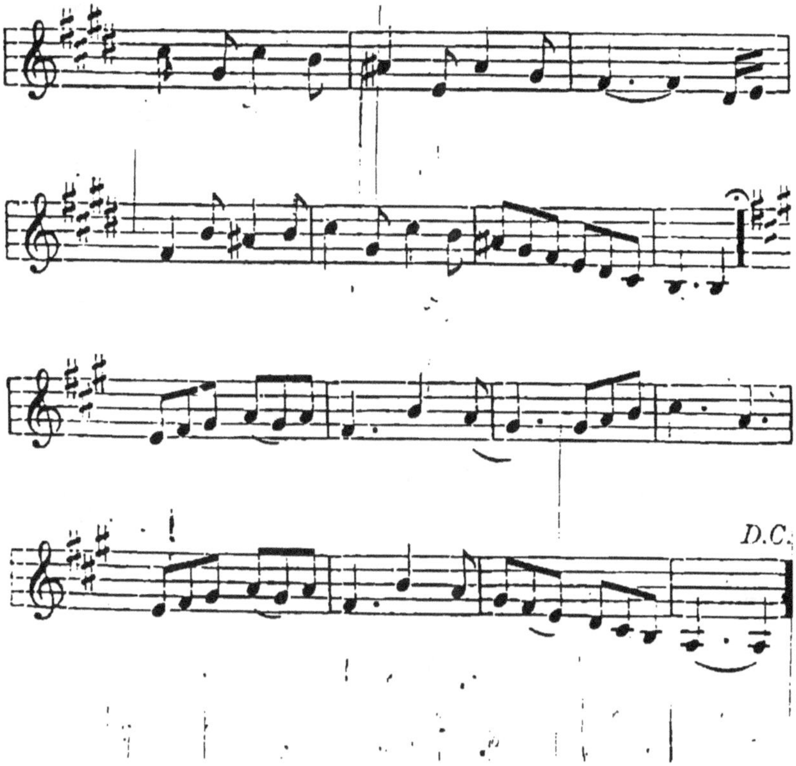
D.C.

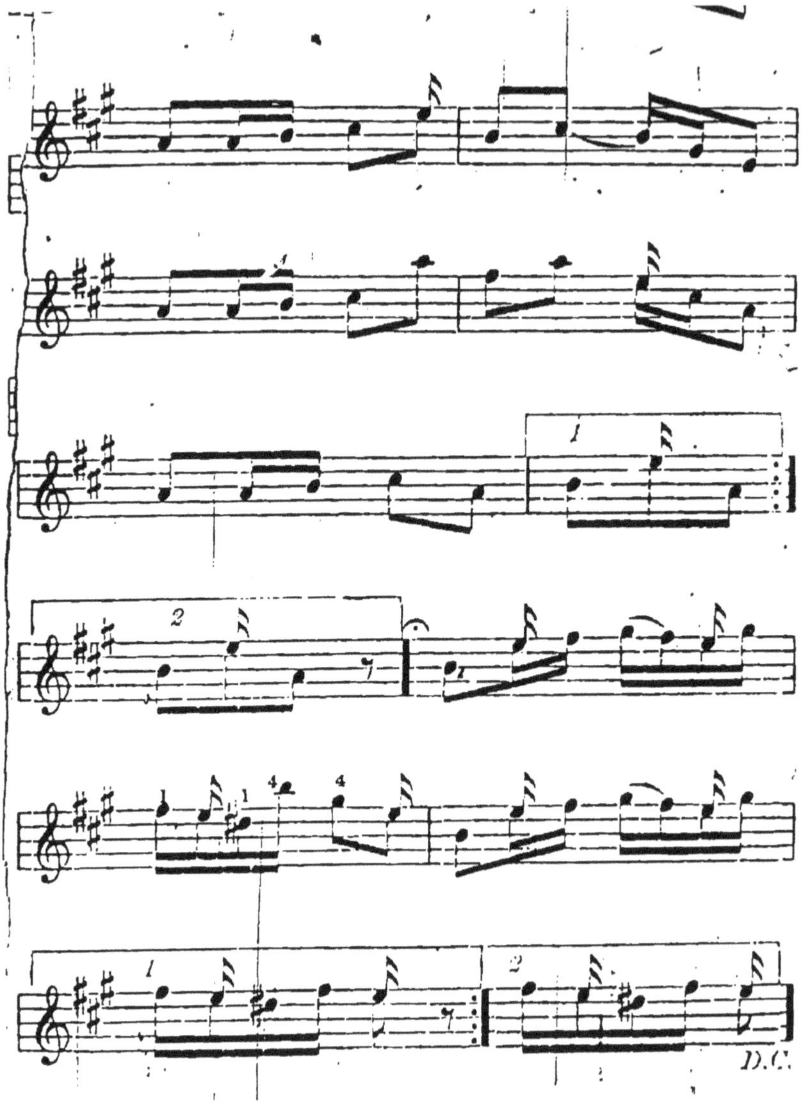
D.C.

DOC GRAHAM'S REEL.

GEO. W. SPENCE.

THE MORNING STAR SCHOTTISCHE.

Tune Bass to B. S. S. S.

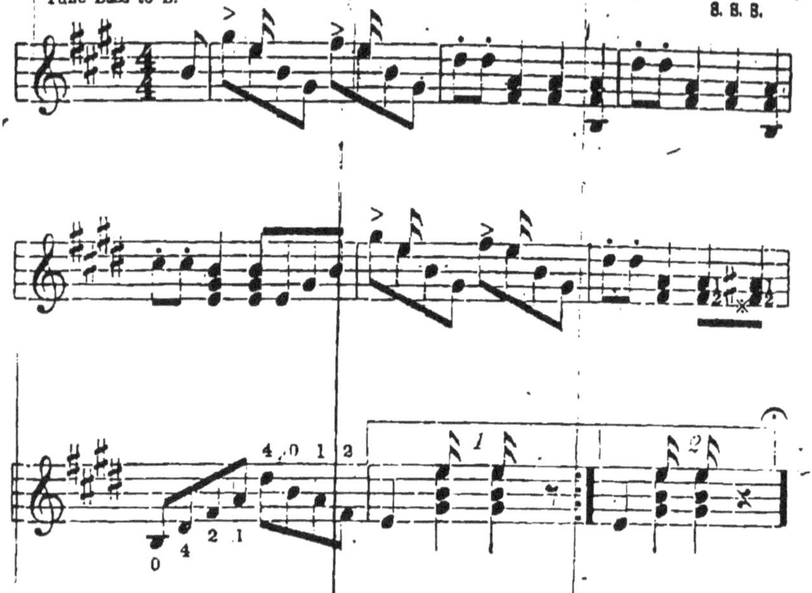

2d Pos. Bar.

ALBANY REEL.

ED. H. HULSE.

THE WAGON JIG.

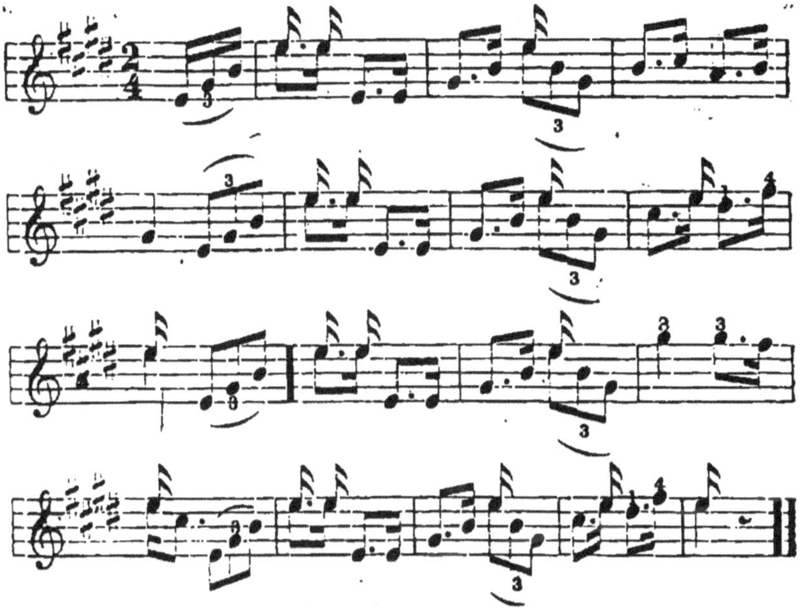

RAKISH HIGHLANDMAN.

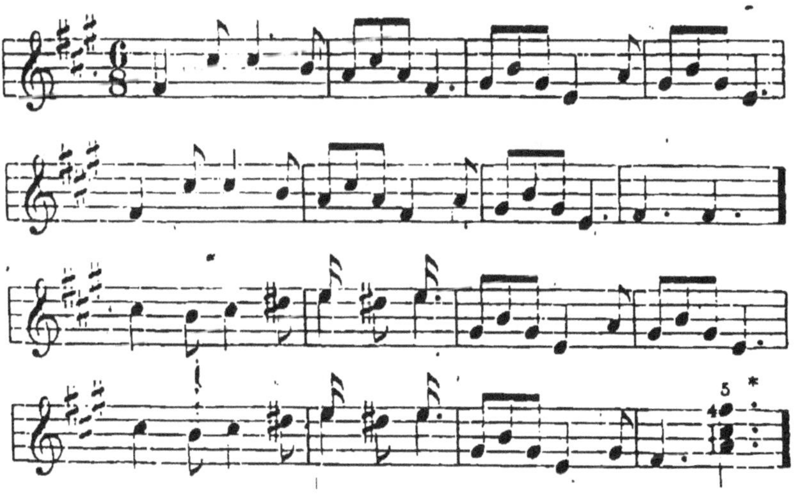

HOME, SWEET HOME AND VARIATIONS.

EASY ARRANGEMENT.

HOME, SWEET HOME. Continued.

Var. 1st.

HOME, SWEET HOME. Concluded.

Var. 2d.

THE CRY OF MARIA.

By C. B. DOOKSADER.

1 No doubt you've all heard Of the great coun-ty fair That takes
2 I got down on my knees And I said, Mis-ter Man, For Ma-
3 The more she would shout, Then the more they cried out; For Ma-

place ev' - ry year at some time; . And
ri - a's sake, won't you take care; . As the
ri - a sat shak - ing with fear; . . . But up

THE CRY OF MARIA. Continued.

I, like the rest, Dressed up in my best, With a
swing went a - past, The girl made a grasp, Caught
went the swing, To the side she did cling: In each

girl on my arm look-ing fine. Oh, the
me by the top of the hair. I
eye you could see a big tear; . Till at

2ᵈ barre.

great Bar - num sho (To ee I did go, For my-
went up and down, (In the dirt rolled a - round. With
last the swing stopped, On the ground she did flop, And

THE CRY OF MARIA. Continued.

self and my girl I did pay, . . . There was
fright then I faint - ed a - way; . . . I came
now I oft hear the folks tell How she

lots of odd things And those round - a - bout swings, Ma-
to with a stare At the swing in mid - air, While Ma-
looked sick and faint And scratched off all the paint, As she

ri - a got in and did say :— . . .
ri - a con - tin - ued to say :— . . .
clung to the swing and did yell :— . . .

THE CRY OF MARIA. Concluded.

Concluded.

REFRAIN.

Oh, Tom! tell 'em to stop!

That was the cry of Ma - ri - a; The.

more she cried whoa, They said let her go! And the

HORACE WESTON'S CELEBRATED POLKA.

HORACE WESTON'S CELEBRATED POLKA. Concluded.

ANN MARIA SUSAN.—BANJO SONG.

ANN MARIA SUSAN. Continued.

1 My love she's join'd the cir - cus, She's an ac - tor in the ring,
2 She was my morn-ing glo - ry, If she on - ly would come back,
3 When first we got acquaint-ed, Oh, she was a soap - fat man,

She's teaching the el - e - phant how to dance, And hip-
I'd buy her a pair of brand new socks To
A - chewing glue for Mrs. Ja Rue, Who

ANN MARIA SUSAN. Concluded.

know   I'll   nev - er   her . more;   She's
pound   of   cheese   and   bar'l   of   fleas   And
now   she's   get - ting   wealth - y,   and   She's

trav' - ling now   by   rail,   And   get-ting two dollars a
ride   her round in a   hack,   My   Ann Ma - ri - a
left   me   all   for - lorn;   I   hope she will die, or get

day,   my boys,   For scrubbing the mon - key's tail.
Su - san, from The   town   of   Kala - ma - zack.
ramm'd in the eye With a rhi - nos - or - 𝛿rus - es' horn.

A BRIEF SKETCH OF THE

LIFE OF S. S. STEWART,

Maker of the Celebrated Banjos.

BY H. P. WAYNE.

SWAIM STEWART, the subject of this sketch, was born in Philadelphia, January 8th, of the year 1855, and although young in years, is already made for himself a name in the musical world. His passion for music made itself manifest at an extremely early age, and he was placed under the charge of a music master in his native city, his instrument at that time being the violin. Having also much mechanical talent, his parents provided him with a work-shop and with suitable tools, and he was wont to occupy himself for several hours daily in the construction of toy fiddles, guitars, mechanical figures, and various other contrivances. In those days young Stewart had conceived no idea of the banjo, never having seen or heard one; and, indeed, there was little about the banjo of that day to attract any one. As he grew from childhood to boyhood his mania for musical instruments increased, and he would buy old and broken violins, and spend many hours in taking them apart and studying their construction and repairing them. He would read with eager delight all books upon the subject he could lay his hands upon, and was never weary of searching public libraries and second-hand book stores for old works relating to his hobby. The experience thus gained he deems the stepping-stone to his success as a maker of **Improved Banjos.**

At fifteen years of age, it is said, he first conceived the idea of becoming a banjo player. He first heard the instrument at one of the minstrel halls, and before long purchased his first banjo, which was a common affair, with ash rim and tack head. A very few days was sufficient to disgust him with this instrument, and it was promptly discarded, and a new one of very elaborate finish purchased at one of the music stores. With this instrument, young Stewart made some progress, though, having no teacher, he was obliged to follow his own ideas, guided by his musical knowledge. The instrument, at best was a very poor one, and should have remained to stand comparison with the one of his own make which he is using at this writing, I fear its claims to being called an instrument at all would be very meagre. As time passed on, young Stewart began to study the construction of the **banjo, and** look into the history of instrument. He purchased all the printed books treating upon the instrument that he could obtain, and discovered what many others now have observed, that the **art of banjo playing and banjo making** was in its infancy. In fact, the banjo stood where the violin had stood centuries ago, when it was called the "devil's instrument." He thereupon began to make experiments, with the idea of improving the tone of the banjo. Hearing that the instruments of a certain maker in New York were held in great esteem by professional players, he soon purchased one of those instruments, which had a maple wood rim, covered with German silver, and a neck of walnut. This instrument, he saw at once, was a great improvement over the former one in appearance, and also possessed a much louder and clearer tone. He therefore began applying the rules of acoustics and mechanics, and making various experiments with these instruments, and with others that he afterwards obtained.

In order to improve and perfect his execution upon the instrument he applied for and obtained instruction from many celebrated performers and teachers. As time passed on, becoming interested in various business pursuits, he was obliged to relinquish, in a measure, practice and experimenting, but he still spent much time in studying music and in composing and writing music for the banjo, and occasionally appearing in public as a performer.

By testing the various powers of the **different makes** of banjos, he was forced to acknowledge a lack of *something* in them all. The tone of the best of them would appear *loud* when struck, but the vibration would cease almost instantly; *there was no carrying property* in the **tone.** This fact was always more apparent in a hall than in a room. After studying the matter for a time, Stewart had an instrument constructed precisely after his own ideas, the rim of which was twelve inches in diameter, and composed of a peculiar grade of maple, covered with German silver, and spun at each side over a round wire; the neck was also made a little longer than that of the instruments he had formerly handled. This instrument proved **very powerful** in tone, and *carried well* in a large hall. Encouraged by his success, he renewed his experimenting, in order to add to the tone more **brilliancy and beauty.** He labored hard and spent considerable money, but at last succeeded. He, step by step, discovered that the methods adopted by the various makers in joining the wood and metal for the rims was wrong, and that in many cases the metal covered rims would have been better without the metal. One of the most common processes of making such rims having been to first join the metal and spin it, and then to fit in the wooden hoop and join it. Rims made in this manner could never be **firm** or **solid,** and the instrument must always have a poor tone. Another plan in use by manufacturers was to join

you can procure at a music store, and note the difference—a dead tone, which vanishes almost as soon as struck.

You may ask, Why is it, then, that Stewart charges twenty to thirty-five dollars for a **fine instrument?** I can answer you. If you had to make one of **Stewart's banjos,** by the time you got through with the job you would think such a sum not half sufficient pay for your trouble. Few can realize the immense amount of care required to construct and perfect such an instrument; and a man to be successful in such a business **must have his whole soul in his work.** Banjos cannot be dealt in like so much **hardware or dry goods.**

There are factories in New York State where banjos are manufactured by steam-power in immense quantities, and supplied to the music trade. Such banjos are not in use by **good players,** but are purchased by those *just beginning to learn,* or those who have not the musical ear to distinguish a good tone from a bad one. The reason that you can, perhaps, buy an old **violin** or **guitar** second-hand, and get a good one, is because there have been perfect instruments of this class made for years, and no improvements worth mentioning have been made of late years. Now, as to the **banjo,** the reason you are **sure to be cheated** if you buy an old one, is because the **banjos made up to a very few years ago were not worth anything at all.**

Many ignorant persons have attempted various so-called "*Improvements*" in the banjo, such as closing the back, making instruments of solid metal, etc. All such attempts have resulted in failure, because the persons attempting them were not **scientifically educated, and had never studied acoustics, and consequently knew nothing** of the science of **sound.**

Reader, you may think your old banjo sounds very fine—yes, you may think you have the **champion toned** instrument of your State. Mr. Stewart has hundreds of letters from parties who thought they had the finest banjo *in the world* before they heard one of **Stewart's banjos.**

A prominent music dealer, when asked why he sold such miserable Banjos, said: "*As long as people are fools enough to buy them, I shall keep them.*" The truth must be, that **some people like to be humbugged.**

Only a short time ago, a person went to Mr. Stewart and ordered a banjo made for twenty dollars, but in a day or two he saw one in a music store for fifteen dollars, and not knowing the difference, he purchased it. After spending about five dollars in repairs to the instrument he finally sold it for six dollars, and lost by his foolishness fourteen dollars. But dearly bought experience is always best. A man who has purchased two or three inferior instruments will be better able to appreciate a **good** one when he finds it.

Mr. Stewart has published several books on the banjo, his most successful work being **The Young Banjoist,** a book for young players and learners. Price, $1.00.

Mr. Stewart may be consulted daily, either by letter or in person, at his store, No. 429 North Eighth street, Philadelphia. He has prepared a pamphlet and various circulars treating upon the banjo, which may be had free.

metal ...e exact size of the wooden hoop, and spin on one side only, then to force the wooden hoop inside the metal cover, and spin the other side of the metal afterwards. This plan is also open to grave objections, and cannot obtain the desired result of **tone**. Stewart made this matter, an object of particular study and research, and finally **perfected a system** which, together with mechanical appliances, cannot be surpassed.

But it is not owing altogether to this that he owes the success of his instruments. Without the proper materials from which to construct his instruments, I doubt if any amount of skill could meet the desired end. Here, too, he has the advantage of **practical acoustical knowledge** and experience, and added to that is his knowledge of music, and his experience as a performer upon the instrument.

It is a well known fact that the Banjos of Stewart's make are becoming *the* instrument of the day; they are much sought after and most highly prized by **proficient performers** and **artists,** and the fact is also apparent that *the more they are used and played upon* **the better they become.**

Mr. Stewart has had one great obstacle to combat against in his business, which is the fact that many purchasers are unable to distinguish the tone of a fine instrument from any ordinary one, and in many cases are led to suppose that the instrument which possesses the harshest or loudest tone is the best—not taking into consideration **beauty** of tone or **carrying properties.**

Just as there are some violinists who would be as well satisfied with a common trade fiddle that cost three dollars, as with a fine violin that cost fifty or a hundred dollars. There are, of course, a great many banjo players who possess artistic taste, and who know how to appreciate a fine toned instrument, and such artists are Mr. Stewart's customers. These persons generally patronize him after having purchased inferior instruments elsewhere, and having been swindled before, they prefer to pay a **fair price** and get a good, reliable instrument direct from the maker. It is a very absurd idea which some beginners possess that any sort of a cheap rattletrap of a Banjo is **good enough to learn on.** The reason why a great many start to learn and then abandon it is because they have such miserable instruments, that they become sick of hearing the sound in a very short time. A banjo that loses its tone as soon as the weather becomes a little *damp, is not worth having* at all. I do not mean to say that dampness does not affect the tone, for no instrument sounds as well in damp weather as in clear weather; but a great many banjos lose *all their tone in damp weather*, and the head becomes as soft and flabby as a wet rag. I say most emphatically that such banjos had best be **cast into the sea.**

Mr. Stewart has studied these matters with such diligence and perseverance that he has made many discoveries in the **science of Banjo making,** which are **his secrets**, and will never be revealed. His large Concert Instruments possess the most beautiful tone that has ever been imparted to an instrument, and the **sound carries** so that they have attracted the attention of *eminent musicians* who had previously looked upon the banjo as only fit for negroes. Strike the bass string upon one of these banjos and you find a **clear, full tone,** full of brilliancy and music. Now, attempt to sound the same string upon any banjo which

www.ingramcontent.com/pod-product-compliance
Lightning Source LLC
Chambersburg PA
CBHW021642270326

41931CB00008B/1129